Am I in a Bad RELATIONSHIP?

Am I in a **Bad** RELATIONSHIP?

Dating 101

A Non-Clinician's Guide to Understanding
Dating In the 21st Century

Dwight A. Owens, MD

Library of Congress Control Number: 2012910175
ISBN: Hardcover   978-1-4771-2492-5
                     Softcover   978-1-4771-2491-8
                     Ebook   978-1-4771-2493-2

To order additional copies of this book, contact:
Xlibris Corporation
1-888-795-4274
www.Xlibris.com
Orders@Xlibris.com
113193

Contents

Introduction

I'm a board-certified psychiatrist practicing in Atlanta, Georgia, but in this e-book, consider me a professor of love, introducing you to basic relationship concepts, opinions on why certain relationships—including your own—don't work. I'll share possible solutions to common problems in your love life, and maybe ways to avoid them in the future. Remember, this is a compilation of my personal blog posts and opinions developed over the past several years. Don't forget to visit my site www. AskDrO.com for more in-depth independent study and to submit further questions. I am using my past posts as well as questions from readers to support many of my lesson plans for *Dating 101*. In the online course you will hopefully receive a grade of B+, if not better. The honor roll is reserved for the quintessential lovers in the house.

In your own life, you may have previously been wary of sharing your relationship issues with friends or family members because of the fear of revealing problems between your partner and yourself. However, now you can read this e-book and reflect on your love life in the comfort of a private personal setting. This is not only an opportunity to examine the ABCs of relationships but also an opportunity to corner your current relationship and inspect it from all angles—whether it is in the budding beginning or in its wilted old end. At the end of this e-book, you may very well gain perspective on whether your relationship is healthy enough to repair or if it is too far gone for any attempts at revival.

I was talking to a couple not too long ago, and this couple was having marital problems, so I decided to ask them a few questions to see if I could get a clear understanding of where their marital problems might have begun. My first question was, "Why did you decide to marry each other?" They both began skipping over their own words. In the end, they could give no substantial answer as to why they were in their relationship. Could it be that they are with each other because they are in love with the idea of what a good relationship should be like. Even though they hadn't ever taken the time to properly analyze themselves and figure out if they knew how to build and operate a healthy, functional relationship they may not know.

Many people don't know how to create and maintain a healthy relationship—many don't even know the basics of what makes a good relationship. You may be one of these people. If so, keep this e-book in your back pocket, if possible.

This e-book shows the basics of what makes a good or bad relationship. It guides you in the direction of establishing and maintaining a good relationship, but it cannot and will not do all of the work for your love life. *You* have to be willing to admit the patterns of a bad relationship if you are in one. *You* have to be willing to be respectful and fully cooperative with your partner if you want to be in a functional relationship.

Making a relationship work is difficult, and you can easily end up failing at it, even when you've worked at it diligently. However, I want to reinforce your efforts with good, basic material on how to reach a higher grade in the future.

What Is Dr. O's Definition of Love?

Ten Clues to Help You Recognize When You Are Really in Love:

1. After an argument or slight disagreement, you and your partner usually don't hold a grudge against each other.

2. You enjoy your partner's postwork scent (bad or good).

3. You are willing to have morning sex before a bath.

4. You kiss each other before a toothbrush has been used by either party.

5. You will wait for your love outside in the cold and rainy weather.

6. You don't ever feel obligated to pay your partner's bills.

7. You have sex more than once a day.

8. You will run up your credit card buying gifts because you want to, not because you feel obligated to or out of habit.

9. You will stay home from an important event just to make love to your partner.

10. You will take an extended lunch, outside of work, for midday sex with your partner.

If you can say yes to at least five of the above clues, you are most probably currently in love.

What Type of Relationship Are You in at This Time?

(Dr. O's Definitions)

Commensalism

From my experience as a therapist, this is a relationship between two people in which one person benefits from one partner in many aspects, but the other partner doesn't end 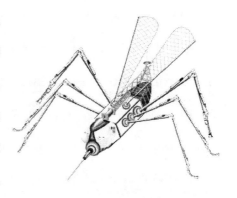 up gaining any emotional, mental, or sexual satisfaction within the relationship. The partner who isn't gaining anything from this relationship doesn't feel emotionally harmed within this relationship; typically, they are the ones who end the relationship. The saying "It's not you, it's me" has never had so much meaning than it does to describe their feelings. The partner who is gaining something from the relationship should not take their partner's rejection as a sign that something is wrong with them. Many times, for a million different reasons, some people just don't end up sharing a mutual bond. In some instances, relationships remain one sided until the person finds a relationship in which the love feels balanced and equally exchanged.

Mutualism

In this relationship, both individuals benefit emotionally, mentally, and, usually, sexually. They do not abuse each other in any way. This type of relationship is typically uncommon, but when it does occur, a couple should make the effort to sustain their strong emotions for each other by making their relationship feel just as new and exciting as it did at the beginning. Ideally, a relationship like this can make for a good, long-lasting marriage or serious relationship. This is the ideal type of relationship for any of us to be in and remain happy over a period of time.

Competition

In this relationship, both individuals are harmed by each other's physical, verbal, or mental abuse. These individuals may be high-strung individuals with large egos and high aspirations for greatness. Perhaps they have gained money from fame or a high-paying profession. Whatever the case may be, they are always in competition with each other to see who will be the most successful at what they do in their vocations. This battle of the mind often evolves into a verbal battle and can even lead to physical battles. In the end, both individuals are morally and emotionally weakened by the war they called their "relationship."

Parasitism

In this type of relationship, one person usually benefits while the other is harmed. Usually, in this relationship, one dominant partner demands to be treated with respect and to have all of their desires met: they call when they need to borrow money or have their partner carry out a favor for them; they fail to take their partner's feelings into consideration; they neglect their partner's emotional needs but expect their partner's full attention. The other partner is not gaining anything from this relationship besides emotional and mental anguish.

However, if they love their demanding partner and think that they can eventually make this relationship work, then they should

1. *set boundaries and parameters to the relationship such as not letting their partner borrow money or request favors that are inconvenient for them,*

2. *continue to enforce those boundaries over time,*

3. *refuse to further tolerate abuse of any kind,*

4. *seek couples counseling to develop resolutions to ongoing problems.*

Hopefully, once the couple has established boundaries and both are in control of the relationship to the point where it is mutually beneficial, they may be satisfied and able to continue to fortify their relationship. If not, other more drastic methods of intervention must be employed. If the dominant partner physically abuses the other partner or threatens them with physical harm when they do not give into their demands, then consider this type of parasitic relationship to be dangerous and physically abusive as well. If you are in one of these relationships, you must find the safest way to leave immediately.

If you feel you are having trouble in your marriage, domestic partnership, or committed relationship, we can help! Start by going to our website www.AskDrO.com.

Premature Infatuation

Let's say you meet someone, fall in lust, and spend the winter having a fling. However, what was supposed to last for a brief season ends up developing into a more serious relationship that crawls into the blooming spring, then the sweltering summer, then toward the chilly fall, and eventually, you and your partner say the three magic  words: *I Love You.* You start to discuss moving in together and becoming exclusive. Perhaps your relationship has the potential to be a long-term one. Perhaps it doesn't. Whether the former or the latter, here are a few clues you can use to detect "premature infatuation," otherwise known as falling in love *way* too fast, which can lead to an equally fast breakup.

- **Using the "I Feel Like I've Known You All My Life" line**

  If it's been under a year, and you or your partner says this line, it might be worth planning an escape route out of this relationship. Sure, you or your partner may feel like you've known the other your whole lives, but not only are you or your partner trying to convince yourselves that you two have some sort of fairy-tale connection, you have fallen victim to the psychological effects of being in love. You have a warped sense of reality—the reality being that you and your partner *have not* known each other your whole lives and *cannot* yet accurately tell how well you will work as a couple.

- **The No-Fly-Zone Approach to Meeting Parents**

  No truly devoted man or woman you are in a relationship with will turn down the opportunity to see where you get your dashing looks and sparkling personality. If your partner has attempted proposing to you several times but plays games whenever you mention meeting your family, you may want to think twice about continuing the relationship with him/her. He/she has obviously not thought of why they want to marry you or if you can work as a couple. Plus, have you forgotten that they don't even make an effort to meet your family? Consider your partner as being high or intoxicated. It is the "high of love" that drives him/her to offer such an irrational proposal of marriage or moving in together without first allowing the relationship to further develop. This development is essential so that both of you can analyze it and predict whether or not you will be able to work as a couple in the future.

- **"Mass" Confessions**

  This is a tricky one; some will confess their love because they truly love you. Others will confess their love to the masses, so that when you call your friends about "the one who went ballistic on their ex-lover," you end up looking like the boy who cried wolf. Watch out for this one, because it is more prevalent than you think.

- **Strength in Numbers**

  Most of the time, if your close friends and family are telling you the *same exact thing*, such as it's too soon for you to move in with your partner or get married or lend him/ her large amounts of money, then no matter how you *feel*, it would be wise to listen to them and try to think about your relationship rationally, instead of with the lust and excitement you're currently feeling.

- **The "Deaf" Syndrome**

    If it seems like the *only* decent communication between you and your partner occurs when you're having sex, this is definitely a red-flag situation. Not only are you moving too fast, but you are confusing real love with lust. You and your partner should be able to speak to each other within a nonsexual context and with mutual respect for each other's opinions. If you find that you can only get along with your partner between the sheets, then it's likely that in the long-run, you won't be waking up next to them at all.

- **Abacus**

    You want your new love to work, and you admire couples whose relationships have endured over long periods of time. However, if your partner habitually brings up dollar amounts, months, days, etc. in regards to your relationship, you in turn should calculate how many seconds it'll take you to run away!

What are other suggestions or ways you can tell if a relationship is moving too fast? Share your thoughts on our blog! Start by going to our website www.AskDrO.com

Love Roller-Coaster

Dear Sad Lover,

How many times has your partner cheated on you and you found out about the infidelity? Or how many times has he/she hit you and/or humiliated you in front of the children? How many times have you borrowed money to pay the bill/mortgage that your partner said they would take care of last month? Has he/she always answered no to your frequent suggestions of going to see a couples' therapist? Finally, how many times have you left your partner and said you would *not* go back to an abusive, one-sided relationship with this selfish person but did anyway?

If you've answered yes too many times to any of these questions, you are taking a hellish ride on a "love roller coaster." The emotions you have regarding your partner and relationship—the guilt about breaking up your family if you leave or disappointing people who think you and your partner are perfect; fear that your partner will physically or emotionally harm you as revenge for leaving; or hope that your love can work "this time"—all these force you to be indecisive about finally ending your dysfunctional relationship. Upon realizing that this dizzying love roller coaster has been making you ill, you probably want some advice on how to safely let go of it.

Follow these four steps:

1. Make a firm decision that you *must leave* your partner.
2. *Choose* a date to escape from your relationship and don't change that date. If you fear for your safety, have a trusted friend or police officer escort you from your home.
3. *Deal* with your subsequent guilt, self-loathing, and depression with a mental health specialist, *not* with your friends who are not properly trained to handle the effects of grief.
4. And finally, *"Just let it go!"*

Yes, I realize that it *is not* easy to let go of someone that you have been intimate with or who you may still love, *but stop* being a prisoner in your own home or world!

Sincerely yours,

Dr. O.

You Can't Make Me Over

Whether it's "I love you" or "I wish I never met you," words can command emotions. Couples often argue and become emotional over differing viewpoints or  preferences. Despite the anger they may have previously been feeling, these arguments and confrontations are usually short term, and people try to reconcile their differences with their partners. But what if your own partner doesn't cooperate when you're trying to make up with him/her and mend your emotions after an argument? What if he/she remains idle, as if amused by your attempts to better your relationship? Remember this simple rule: *you cannot change the behavior of anyone who doesn't want to change!* Dragging someone through a relationship, or trying to create an environment to which they're not responding will only wear you out.

Also, despite your partner's less-than-agreeable qualities, sometimes *you* might be the reason for your own emotional downfall. Reevaluate your actions after a simple disagreement or argument. Do you find healthy distractions after a fight, or do you run straight to the phone to tell someone who may in turn reprimand your partner or force him/her to make up with you? Do *you* force your partner to talk about their feelings or apologize to you right after an argument? Sometimes the way you react when communicating with your partner after a fight could be pushing your partner away. But on the other hand, if your partner won't contact you for an unreasonable period of time after an argument or doesn't want to make up with you after you've reached out to them, then that's when you know that you are in a relationship with a person who is content with holding grudges. Such a person may also be okay with punishing you for having the nerve to make them angry in the first place.

You may have to reconsider your relationship if you find that

- *you're always the first to call your partner after a fight;*
- *you find yourself having to change or alter one side of your personality to keep from getting into recurrent arguments with your partner;*

- *your 50/50 partnership is slowly becoming 60/40, then 70/30, and so on, until you are feeling like you are doing all of the work;*
- *every subject you discuss with your partner results in his/ her defensive behavior; and*
- *many of your partner's desires for the relationship are based solely on what he/she wants.*

Facebook Follies and Internet Hookups: Real and Imagined

Like . . .

Unlike . . .

Friend . . .

Delete Friend . . .

Do any of these commands

sound familiar to you?

Technology has made the

world an easier place. We can

connect with almost anyone in

the world through email, phone, the internet, or television. For

this reason, people have developed an impatience for patience.

The "right now" is what people want—a burger delivered in under

a minute at a fast food joint, express delivery of items bought over

a high-speed internet connection . . . and now, love.

Thanks to various dating sites, you can now get love on the fly.

The process is simple: *find a random "hot" friend in your area,*

chat with them for a minute to discuss intentions, figure a time and location . . . and finally . . . meet. It's free, it's fast and can be perfectly fun and safe if you are single and are not deceiving your partner. You should not cheat on your partner with someone you've met online. However, when it comes to social networking sites (and potential dating sites) like Facebook, you may be putting your relationship in danger (if you are in one) or risking your social skills (in exchange for technological entertainment) with continuous visitations. When you are depressed or upset, you may seek comfort in many things: food, television, music, and now, Facebook. Facebook and the other previously mentioned items are what mental health professionals consider "stimulants," which encourage emotional regularity. If your partner makes you angry or stressed, and there's no communication within that relationship, you might retreat to sites like Facebook for comfort, and it may act as a drug to boost your mood.

The problems that come along with cruising Facebook in an attempt to cheer you up is what I call Facebook follies. If an attractive Facebook friend is usually available for chatting at your most vulnerable moments, who's to say that you won't slip up and develop a real or imaginary relationship with him/her? If your "friendliness" with this person does develop into an actual, physical relationship, well then of course you know that this is wrong, since you are deceiving your own partner. Though less extreme than actual cheating, if you are in an imaginary relationship with your attractive Facebook friend, it is unhealthy because you are attaching your feelings to someone who has no obligation to be with you or ensure your happiness within this imagined "relationship."

Other Facebook follies include developing the social-media-hookup "high," which can turn into a possible addiction to social networks and contacting and communicating with others only through social networks. This can cause erratic or panicky behaviors when your computer or the internet isn't functioning properly and you can't log onto any of these social sites. Even worse, if you are always communicating through a social network, your social skills can wane, with the possible result of social awkwardness when you don't have a media device in your control. This factor, combined with cheating on your partner with a real or imagined lover, can lead to a breakup or divorce.

When relationship or marital problems arise, instead of looking for a quick fix of cruising the internet or sites like Facebook,

1. *Breathe in and out, deeply and slowly.* You must assess the pros and cons of your current relationship situation,

then proceed to take responsible action to resolve the issue with your partner.

2. Also, *keep a journal*. Writing in your journal after an argument with your partner can help you release some of your anger and frustration. Since you are expressing your negative emotions in a private way, you'll less likely hurt your partner's feelings with words or actions that you may later regret.

3. Once you have written in your journal, sometimes it helps to *discard the written page*. In this way, you are *throwing out* your frustrations, and you're expressing yourself without the use of a media tool, plus your partner won't have the chance to find this written page and become hurt or offended by your words regarding him/her.

Have you found this blog entry to be helpful? Let me hear your thoughts and comments, or even your suggested coping methods may help another reader!

AskDrO.com is a great supporter of healthy mental maintenance. Go to our website www.AskDrO.com. *We are here for you!*

I'm in Love with My Best Friend

Do we, as a society, consider the words *lover* and *friend* to be the same? This is a tough one, being that your lover should first be your friend. However, if you are supposedly "just friends" with someone, many times, lust is factored into the "me and you" equation and that can signal trouble. If you are single or are in a relationship and are in love with a friend who may or may not be romantically available, ask yourself the following questions:

1. *Am I sexually satisfied in my current relationship with my own partner?*

2. *What can my friend potentially offer me that my current partner can't?*

3. *Are you willing to let go of your current relationship to pursue a romantic relationship with your friend?*

4. *Do my friend and I spend time in potentially romantic places (movie theaters, dimly lit restaurants, or hot, dark dance clubs)?*

5. *Have I always had these feelings for my friend?*

6. *In the past, has my friend tried to make a move (leaning in for a kiss, holding my hands, etc.) but hesitated?*

7. *If I'm single and my friend is single, what do I have to lose if I make a move?*

Another important point here is that many people come into my office not even knowing what forms of foreplay or positions their significant other likes. They don't even know the sensitive points/areas on their partner's body. When you have bad sexual chemistry in your relationship, you may begin looking at those close to you (such as a good friend) as sexual prey. If it's just about sex, make sure that you fix the problems in your current relationship before finding solutions in someone else's pants.

When it comes to interacting with a friend you have feelings for while you are in an active relationship, please be cautious. You have to be very careful where you take your so-called platonic friends. Remember low lighting, wine, and linen tablecloth may transport you and your friend to a different place where you are no longer friends but are *now* intimate partners. As we mature, we may be able to handle our impulses more. However, if you do fine dine with your friend, be sure that you each pay for your own meals and stay out of dimly lit corners (i.e. bedrooms). If your friend is also in a relationship, then I think you both know how bad an idea it would be to pursue a relationship behind your partner's back. Your relationship with your friend would most likely be built on lust or the false belief that they will relieve the problems you are having in your current relationship. This relationship with your friend would be based only on lies. Moreover, if your partner finds out about this, it could possibly lead to the loss of the current long-term relationship you have with an existing partner.

If you are single but want to pursue a relationship with a friend who is also available, remember, you may have a lot to lose, such as your friendship, especially if you two end up dating but break up because you're not a good fit. You may also lose some pride and self-esteem if your friend doesn't feel the same way about you. They may even distance themselves from you, because they now feel awkward being around someone who they know has feelings for them, and they have no romantic feelings in return. Some people simply want you to stay as their friend. If you know that this is the case, do not push it. Don't tell them what a great couple the two of you would make. You may very well push a great person out of your life by being so desperate.

With all that said, if your friend is single and you sense that you're romantic feelings are mutual, initiate a conversation with him/her. If you meet any resistance, retreat and attempt to resume the position of a friend. You might be a little surprised or hurt, but you will get through it eventually. If he or she is willing to transfer your friendship into a relationship, and both of you are aware of the risks of losing your friendship, then go for it with caution. I wish you two the best of luck!

Enough said,

Dr. O.

Triple Threat

Many of us have fallen prey, at one time or another, to the dreaded love triangle. I am sure you are wondering what I consider to be an active love triangle. Well, here is my definition: a love triangle occurs when *there is an intimate relationship knowingly or unknowingly, between three individuals, all of whom may or may not have been aware of being in a triangle at the time it began.*

In this triangle, you may be married or in a committed relationship with someone and are cheating on your significant other; you may be the one being cheated on without even knowing about it; or you may be a single person who is either aware or unaware that your partner is already in a supposedly "committed relationship." Some people even have sex with their married co-workers or bosses at work, which puts them at risk of being terminated due to acting inappropriately in a work environment. However, what usually happens is that when this relationship dissolves, so does the comfort level on the job.

Lust and sex can be addictive for many people. However, if you are in a serious commitment or if you stay sexually involved with someone that you know for a fact has a girlfriend/boyfriend or is married, you are putting yourself at risk for emotional, mental, and possible physical pain.

Yes, there are people who feel safe in relationships with people who are already involved with someone else. They will say, "I know exactly what to expect in this relationship, so there are really no surprises or high expectations between me and my partner." You might even be one of those people who agree, and yes, you're allowed to have an opinion. However, will you have a change of opinion when I tell you this type of relationship's possible side effects? Here they are:

- **STDs**

  Whether you are the married person in this relationship or the single one, if you and your partner have unprotected sex, you have to remember that your partner could be having unprotected sex with other people (his/her wife or husband or additional lovers). Just who are all of those *other* people they are having sex with? Are *they* using condoms? Sure, you may demand that you and your partner use a condom during sex, which will greatly reduce STDs passed through genital contact, but condoms don't always work—tearing can occur or the condom can be less effective in protecting you against STDs passed through fluids from the genitalia. Also, if you haven't used a dental dam during oral sex, you may be at risk for contracting any STDs passed from the genitalia to the mouth. Who knows who else your partner has been with?

• **Unwanted Pregnancies**

What if you and your partner don't always use a condom? If you're a woman and you become pregnant, you may want to keep this child, but your lover may not want to keep the baby. If he is married or has a serious girlfriend, don't fool yourself into thinking that what he wants to do is end his long-term, steady relationship with his partner to be with you and your unborn child. Also, if you don't have health insurance, you may not even have enough money to get an abortion. Will you be ready to take care of a child if you don't even have enough money, ironically enough, to get rid of one? Can you see yourself actually giving up your child for adoption? Are you prepared for your partner's refusal to leave his/her partner for you and your new child? If you are a man who has taken on another female partner in addition to your wife or girlfriend, are you prepared to be in a situation where you get a woman pregnant and she wants to keep your baby and legally bind you to take care of it? Wouldn't this ruin your serious relationship or even ruin you financially if your budget is not ready to include a new child?

- **Ending of Your Serious Relationship**

  If you have a boyfriend or girlfriend or are married and your significant other finds out about your infidelity, you may find yourself shoved down a road leading to a breakup or divorce.

- **Abuse and Neglect**

  Because you may not be the "main" man or woman in your partner's life, do not be surprised if you are often neglected—he/she forgets your birthday, he/she cancels your dates at the last minute, etc. Also, since you are not the most important person in your partner's life, they may not feel inhibited when it comes to abusing you verbally or physically, seeing as you and whatever relationship you have with them is not their main priority. Whether they're having problems at work or harboring frustration and resentment regarding their family life or their main spouse, lashing out at you—someone they just might consider a plaything—can be a way for your partner to release his/her anger.

- **Depression and Suicidal Ideation**

  If you put an unrealistic expectation upon your partner such as telling them that they should spend more time with you in spite of having a family of their own or pressuring them to leave the person that they are in a committed relationship with, then their refusal of your expectations may cause you to feel rejected, guilty, vulnerable, depressed, and maybe even suicidal. Vice versa, a partner who puts unrealistic expectations on *you* may end up also feeling all of these negative emotions if you refuse him/her as well.

- **Physical Aggression**

  Since love triangles are often hidden from unwitting partners, the partner who has finally found out about their partner's infidelity can lash out in a violent way that targets them and/or the person they are cheating with at that time.

If you are in a love triangle, I realize that it may not be easy to break out of this relationship, since you likely have invested emotionally in this partner. However, I am hoping that we get a couple of testimonies that prove it can be done. Can you share with others how you've successfully pulled away from your love triangle?

Go to our website www.AskDrO.com. There, I can also provide you with advice on how to break yourself from a threesome relationship.

"I Think It's Time We See Other People..."

Ways to Effectively Break out of a Bad Relationship

Whether your relationship is an abusive one or just plain bad, when you want to end it:

1. make a firm decision to break up with your partner and stick to it! Failure to do this can lead to feelings of guilt, low self-esteem, and depression because you have not completed what you intended;

2. significantly reduce your cell phone interactions with your partner over time. Remember you want the relationship to be over . . . not to linger over the phone;

3. remove his/her pictures from your office, keychain, or home;

4. don't listen to love ballads during the critical breakup period. This may lead to feelings of longing for the "old days" when you and your partner were in love. It may also

lead to depression, as love songs may remind you that other people are in love while you are in the middle of breaking off your relationship;

5. *do not* participate in makeup sex with your partner during the breakup period. This can lead to further attachment and make it difficult to break off the relationship for good;

6. there is no need for *any* face-to-face interactions during the breakup period (this includes lunch dates or having dinner together). You may easily begin performing the same routines with this partner until you gradually find yourself right back in a relationship with them!

7. return *all* of his/her personal property in a public area (i.e. a shopping center, at a public park, in a crowded area of town, etc.);

8. stop calling his/her parents like you would when you two were together;

9. try *not* to fall asleep with your ex on your mind.

How to Survive After a Bad Relationship

Surviving a bad relationship may not be easy, but this task has been accomplished by many. After a breakup, you may feel depressed because you could not make your relationship work with the person you love, and you may feel guilty for having left your relationship/marriage if there are children involved or meddling family members who wanted you and your partner to stay together. If you've just exited a relationship that was abusive in any way, remember that you are doing the right thing by having left him/her behind. In the end, this relationship would have resulted in your partner killing you emotionally, mentally, spiritually or, in the worst case, physically.

Now, whatever the reason for your break-up, *you will have to work on accepting this new change in your life and letting your partner, your family's expectation, your guilt, your depression and your doubts go!*

Survival Tips:

1. *Promise yourself that things will be better soon.*

2. *Seek professional help if you really need it.*

3. *Self-heal (without the use of drugs, sex, or alcohol) by doing things such as attending a service at a place of worship or meditating at home.*

4. *Engage in physical exercises such tennis, jogging, biking, swimming, weightlifting, etc., which will release chemicals in your brain to reduce your stress and depression.*

5. *Eat right! Omega-3 fatty acids, tryptophan, vitamin D, or B vitamins in foods like spinach, milk, salmon, bananas, whole grains, soy, turkey, and even chocolate don't just taste good, but they stimulate the brain and make us physically happy too.*

This week, take the opportunity to perform a *self-evaluation*. If you have been having sleepless nights, crying spells or flashbacks from a previous bad relationship, please go to our website <u>www. AskDrO.com</u> or give us a call at the office (404-575-4785) to schedule an appointment.

Ten Ways To Be a Better Lover in Your Next Relationship

1. *Understand* who *you* are as an individual before making any *new* love connections.

2. *Stop* being *dependent* on your mates (past or present) for an *identity*, because you need to develop your true *identity* yourself.

3. Recognize your *personal weaknesses* and conquer each of them on your own. Don't take old baggage from a past relationship and plunk it down in a *new* relationship.

4. Develop your own set of *goals* first and then corroborate with your partner on mutual goals for your relationship (i.e. what you expect from each other, how you will decide on fulfilling these expectations, etc.).

5. In the beginning of your relationship, be open and honest about your *needs for intimacy and sex.*

6. Remove the telephone numbers of all of your former intimate partners from your phone book (PDA, iPhone, etc.) *before* you enter into a new commitment with someone.

7. Let your partner know early in the relationship where *you* want this new relationship to go.

8. Don't *reveal* your vulnerabilities to your partner until you are sure you can trust them with such sensitive information.

9. Always *be true to yourself.* Don't change your personality, physical appearance, or behavior for any man or woman.

10. If you are serious about this *new* commitment, then don't lead other people into believing you're single or that you are interested in them. Lest they get any ideas, mention your boyfriend/girlfriend, to give them a reality check.

Do you agree with my recommendations above? Did I (AskDrO) leave off any key concepts or components? Are there any that are essential ingredients for the success of a new relationship that this Atlanta psychiatrist forgot? Help Dr. O. on this one by letting me hear from you on this crucial issue . . .

Hit up that website and share . . . www.AskDrO.com

Seven Daily Romantic Tips/Activities for You and Your Partner to Keep the Relationship Alive

Whatever activities you decide to engage in with your partner, make sure these activities have the potential to bring you two emotionally, mentally, spiritually or sexually closer together. Here are some tips:

1. **Sunday:** Brunch at a new restaurant that neither of you have ever visited.

2. **Monday:** Surprise your partner with flowers! This way, a Monday is not just another start to a long, boring workweek, but a promise of more romantic things to come later in the week.

3. **Tuesday:** Sweat together! Jog in the park side-by-side—no iPods allowed. You'll be keeping yourselves in shape, boosting your endorphin levels (certain chemicals in your brain make you happier!), and most important of all, you'll

be spending time together. You can also go for a walk or a swim at the beach with your partner.

4. **Wednesday:** Make popcorn, select a free movie on one of your network television channels, and watch the movie with your partner on the living room sofa/floor.

5. **Thursday:** Go to an art museum or go see a live rock band or hip-hop group at a local music venue. The mall can be a last resort too.

6. **Friday:** Full total body massages with the appropriate oil for your partner's skin type.

7. **Saturday:** Cook a fancy dinner with your partner and eat together in your own backyard, drive out of town to a new place or go to the local amusement parks or ice-cream shop. Attend a matinee in the afternoon or a drive-in movie late night.

Keep in mind that these tips are just ideas to get you started—you and your partner should try to come up with activities that fit your schedule or ones that both of you might enjoy.

Is Your Relationship Headed for the Rocks?

Ten Reasons Relationships Can Fail:

1. Poor Communication

- Many couples have problems with communication. You and your partner have to be open and honest about all of the issues that come up in your relationship.

2. Infidelity

- The grass looks greener on the other side, but it is usually withered. In addition, if your mate finds out about your infidelity, they may just get back at you by sleeping with someone else. How can a relationship grow when so much mistrust dwells inside both of you? You and your partner may no longer trust the other to be the "soul mate" you'd hoped to spend the rest of your lives with, and that is the beginning of many problems to come.

3. Cash-Flow Problems

- Where there is *no* money, usually there is *no* peace. I don't care how much a person loves you or how good the sex maybe, lack of funds usually leads to trouble, since you'll spend a lot of time discussing or arguing about spending too much or sacrificing something to pay the bills. If you have children in a relationship, the problem is worsened because, well, children are expensive! Children require extra food, extra clothes for their growing bodies, school expenses, toys, books, entertainment expenses, and the list goes on and on.

4. Irregular sex dates

- Please, please, be sure that you are sexually compatible. Guess what: if your partner wants to have sex two to three times a week and you don't, then he/she may be tempted to seek pleasure elsewhere. It's important to be on the same page sexually and to be vocal about your sexual needs.

5. Premature ejaculation

- This is a terrible problem for a lot of men. Ladies, if you require longevity during sex, don't be afraid to admit to your partner that this problem will become an issue for you in the long run. If you choose not to be open with your partner, you will only become more frustrated over time and perhaps seek satisfaction from another person.

6. Excessive Working

- While you and your partner may like your jobs, don't make work your life and forget about pleasing and being there for each other emotionally. Workaholics can be boring or preoccupied. They sometimes experience problems in the bedroom, secondary to fatigue and work-related stress.

7. Having a Sad Pal

- A friend who is bitterly single or in a bad relationship can certainly be a problem. Misery loves company, so your friend may convince you that something is terribly wrong with your partner or your relationship when there is no real issue. Watch out for that negative friend who is always in your ear.

8. Lack of Intimacy

- The actual act of sex doesn't interest people all of the time, so holding, caressing, kissing, and so on can be quite fun when done with the one you love. If someone isn't getting this kind of affection from their partner on a regular basis, they may start to feel neglected or that they are only being used for sex.

9. Television/Football

- Remember, don't put sports or entertainment or the television before your partner whether it comes to sex, having a conversation, having a meal at the dinner table, or going out to enjoy a night in the city.

10. Unemployment

- Unemployment is so unattractive. Brothers: you have to get a job, or at least be actively searching for one, in order to get a woman who'll respect you and consider you a man who can take care of a family in the future.

Ten Ways to Tell if Your Partner Is Cheating on You

1. New *lack* of intimacy in the bedroom and other areas of your relationship.

2. Your partner now has an extra *cell phone* that is always locked . . . even worse, you don't have the number to it.

3. He/she applies *fresh cologne or perfume after 8:00 p.m. when leaving home.*

4. Your lover now has a *new and odd work schedule* (i.e. unusual deadlines and work hours).

5. He/she becomes *irritable* when you ask where they've been for an extended period of time.

6. Your partner now wants *to wash their own laundry separately from yours.*

7. They request the very popular wish, "I want some 'me' time."

8. He/she is *unusually quiet during sex.*

9. Lack of *orgasms or climax* during sex.

10. Your partner begins to *leave the room to speak on the phone.*

Bonus: *Excessive texting is always a sign of something possibly bad to come!*

Do you agree with the signs or not? Hit me up on the blog and let me know what you think!

What's your current love mental status? Take Dr. O's Mental Evaluation Screening to assess your current mental status. Start by going to our website <u>www.AskDrO.com</u>

Ten Ways to Tell if Your Partner Is Cheating on You (Part II)

If you answered yes to at least five of the above points, here are the next steps:

1. First, take the test over to see if you get the same score.

2. If the score is still *positive* (five or more) it is now time to *develop a plan of action.*

3. Stop all unprotected sex for now. If he or she asks why, be real and disclose your thoughts.

4. Check all of your personal assets in case you have to move out. Relocation may be necessary for one or both parties if violence becomes a factor. Also, never ever have only just a combined bank account!

5. If you feel that your friends will spread gossip about your relationship, *do not,* I repeat, *do not disclose your*

business to friends. If you have a physician or someone who is bound by law to maintain confidentiality, discuss the issue with them.

6. If you're Christian and have a pastor who is professional and caring, you may want to talk to him/her.

7. Confront your partner *cautiously* about your suspicions.

8. If he/she becomes angry or agitated and refuses to speak with you about the subject any further, then this is usually a "confirmatory" sign that they are cheating.

9. If he/she accuses you of being crazy or overreacting, and you are sure that you are not, they are likely trying to use reverse psychology to trick you into believing that they are innocent.

10. If they seem shocked, concerned, and hurt by the accusation, give them the benefit of the doubt. However, keep your eyes and ears open just to be 100 percent sure. You may want to even reevaluate your relationship. If you're worried or suspecting that your partner is cheating, do you really trust him/her? Can you see yourself spending the rest of your life with someone you'll again suspect of cheating in the future?

If you need more help dealing with relationship issues, feel free to consult your local mental health professional and or schedule an appointment at our office in Atlanta.

Ten Warning Signs That You May Be a Sex Addict

The following list is not based on any scientific study, just practical notations made from my professional observations in the psychiatric office setting.

Please Take This Test When Alone.

1. You require more than several *sexual episodes* per day.

2. You have *pornography* in several different places (i.e. home, school locker, and/or work).

3. *Both* male and female genders turn you on.

4. Your significant other often seriously calls you a freak when it comes to sex and intimacy.

5. You have had more than one sexually transmitted disease (STD) in the past.

6. You have been *caught having sex* in culturally inappropriate places (i.e. cars, churches, dressing rooms, etc.).

7. You have had to leave work, school, or a place of worship to *masturbate or have sex.*

8. You are *easily* turned on by *people in power*, such as doctors, lawyers, or pastors.

9. You do not require your partner to *maintain appropriate hygiene* prior to sex.

10. Body odors in certain places turn you on rather than off.

If you answered yes to five or more the above statements, you should seek professional help because this addiction to sex is most likely interfering with your home, work, and/or professional life. It consumes your thoughts and your time to the point where you are not completing tasks that need to get done or you cannot mentally function without sex. Don't be afraid to take action. If your significant other is the one with the sex-addiction problem, you may be in trouble as well, because he/she has the potential to cheat on you with several other people. If you believe you are addicted to sex or your partner is addicted to sex, there is a greater chance of contracting STDs or HIV when unprotected sex is practiced with other people.

If you feel you need help dealing with the possibility of being a sex addict, please visit www.AskDrO.com or consult your nearest mental health professional.

Do you feel that this list was complete? Did I leave anything out? Do you know someone who might be a sex addict, but you are afraid to tell them? Let me hear from you anonymously at my website <u>www.AskDrO.com</u>

STDs in Disguise

Imagine that you have been married or are in a monogamous relationship for two years. Week one, you notice a little irritation while urinating. Week two, you experience a burning sensation when urinating. Week three, you have an actual discharge from your vagina/penis. As a result, you mention this to your partner, and he/she looks surprised and strongly denies having similar symptoms. You have never had a urinary tract infection (UTI) or STD, so you are concerned but not overly worried. You have learned to trust your partner over the past several years. Depression attempts to creep in as you begin to doubt him/her, but you remain confident in your relationship. You are convinced that this is just a normal yeast infection or bacterial infection and nothing more.

When you visit the doctor's office and tell your physician the list of symptoms you have, your physician requests your permission to do a couple of tests. You immediately agree to the urinary analysis and culture. However, you are somewhat reluctant to take any other tests. You share with your physician how wonderful and committed your partner is to you; therefore, you are not convinced that tests looking for any STDs or HIV will find anything. Plus, you really don't want to pay the additional co-pay fees. However, the doctor convinces you to go ahead and test for gonorrhea, chlamydia, and HIV.

The nurse calls you the next day on behalf of your physician. She explains that your physician would like to speak with you face-to-face. You panic and tell the nurse that you want your physician to go ahead and share the results over the phone. Your doctor then confirms that you have gonorrhea and chlamydia. He does not have your HIV-test results back just yet. You will immediately feel betrayed, angry, worried, and overwhelmed—but do not try to harm yourself in any way. If you have not been sexually involved with anyone besides your partner, yet you find out that you have contracted an STD or HIV, your primary lover is most likely the infectious vector.

1. You most definitely should confront him/her about it. Perhaps he/she hasn't had any of the symptoms you've been having, but nevertheless, your partner needs to confirm their status with tests and seek immediate treatment. He/she also needs to inform the partner or partners that he/

she has been sleeping with that they may have an STD and possibly HIV.

2. Also, if you find out that your partner knew he had an STD or HIV but had unprotected sex with you anyway, it is best to consider this relationship a lost cause. Not only has he/she been deceiving you by cheating on you, but he/she has put your physical and emotional health at risk. Time to say goodbye! If you feel that your partner's actions were done deliberately to hurt you, then you may even want to look into pressing charges.

Recycle Emotions

When I looked for a definition for recycled emotions, I quickly discovered that there is no such thing. However, there is a working definition for *recycled,* which is the processing of used materials into new products  to prevent waste of potentially useful materials, reduce the consumption of fresh raw materials, reduce energy usage, reduce air pollution (from incineration of paper or other recyclables) and to reduce water pollution (from land filling) by decreasing the need for "conventional" waste disposal.

Porter, Richard C. (2002). *The Economics of Waste.* Resources for the Future. ISBN 1-891853-42-2, 9781891853425

Here is my newly developed definition for "recycled emotions":

This is a method that involves saving your intimate emotions from a nasty, uncaring partner. If you are in an abusive relationship, the waste of time and emotions should be stopped immediately. You should not waste your precious breath (or cell-phone minutes) by attempting to fix the relationship you have with a control freak that has repeatedly emotionally hurt you, played with your emotions by cheating on you, or, more importantly, physically threatened you.

In essence, you should *reduce* the time and energy you spend trying to fix this "relationship." You should reuse your intimate emotions in someone willing to invest time and energy in *you*. Finally, you should *recycle* your love emotions to prevent wastage of your perfectly healthy, sound, and loving heart.

Dr. O.

Pitfalls to Being in the Wrong Type of Relationships

Physical, Sexual, and Emotional Abuse

Does your partner inflict on you any type of physical pain, whether with their own body parts or with an object? If so, you are in a physically abusive relationship. How about when it comes to sex? Does your partner force you to engage in sexual intercourse or other sex acts by way of emotional manipulation or threats of physical abuse? If so, you are definitely in a sexually abusive relationship. If you're the victim in an emotionally abusive relationship, then your abusive partner likely creates a sustained climate of anxiety in the relationship with verbal insults, dominating behavior (i.e. forbidding you to hang out with friends), and jealous accusations that you are sleeping with or are in love with someone else.

One, two, or even all three of these types of abuse may be present in your current relationship. Any form of abuse is unacceptable at any time. Remember, abuse is the aggressor's fault, *never* your own.

Physical Illness

Frustrations about your relationship can manifest themselves as physical illness and depression. You or your partner may seek help from a medical professional but will find it difficult to be open and honest about the cause of the ailments. The root of many biological diseases (or what psychiatrists call Axis III disorders) lies in underlying stress from conflict. If you're in the wrong type of relationship, unresolved conflicts can certainly manifest themselves as physical illnesses. Hypertension, diabetes, heart attacks, and even annoying skin problems have all been tied to mental stress and emotional conflict from a bad relationship.

Financial Problems

Often, we make financial commitments to the people we thought we'd love forever. Examples of financial commitments would be taking out a new home mortgage or co-signing for cars and credit cards with a boyfriend or girlfriend. I advise that you only get financially involved with a partner after legalizing your relationship through marriage. Day in and day out, I have seen situations where one partner has left the other responsible for all of the debts they've acquired while they had been a couple. As a result, foreclosure on a property and bankruptcy became almost inevitable for the partner left holding the bag. Although with much less frequency, this can also happen in both legal marriages and common-law marriages better known as shacking up.

Pregnancy

More often than not, having a child with a partner you're in a bad relationship with will not make the relationship any better. In fact, a child may only serve to pile more stress on you and your partner as your expenses increase to provide for the child. Make sure that if there is premarital sex in your relationship, there is condom use. Children should not be the casualties of an adult war (i.e. your bitter divorce or separation or breakup). However, if you are intending on having a child with your partner one day, make sure that you strengthen the relationship enough to happily and healthily tolerate a new addition to the union.

If you are a woman in an abusive relationship and have become pregnant by your abusive male partner, he may force you to keep his child. If you are too afraid to leave your partner, not only are you remaining in an abusive relationship, but the unborn child may end up being raised in an environment that is hostile and unhealthy. Is this the type of life you wish for your unborn child? One soiled by fear, pain, and dysfunction?

For women just dating or carrying on a noncommitted sexual relationship with a man, be mindful of the fact that you may become pregnant. What if you are in a dysfunctional love triangle, wherein he is married or has a serious girlfriend and your "relationship" with him will never grow stronger because it is not based on honesty and dual commitment to a common bond? Don't fool yourself into thinking that he will end his long-term marriage just because you are expecting a child. Are you prepared for the possible rejection from your partner when he finds out that you are pregnant? If you are with a man who has taken on another significant female partner, be very cautious.

Alcoholism and Other Substance-Abuse/ Dependence Problems

Being in a wrong type of relationship may have you running to the liquor store or to a drug dealer when you're feeling too stressed to confront the problems between you and your partner. Perhaps you are even being abused in this relationship.

Whatever the issue, drinking or using narcotics as a method of escape from your relationship's problems only works for a little while and is not an effective way of handling any problem. In fact, it often exacerbates problems you may have in your relationship. When you're under the influence of alcohol or drugs, your inhibitions may be lowered as well as your ability to make good judgments. Add to that mix a terrible relationship with a partner you can't get along with, and you may end up doing or saying something that harms your partner. You should not opt for mood-altering substances to ease the pain you're feeling in your relationship. You should take initiative and leave your relationship if it is ruining the very essence of what makes you a lively, caring, and dynamic person.

Divorce

This is the ultimate way that a wrong type of relationship can come to a dramatic end. You reach this conclusion when no other means of bonding (couple's therapy, sex, weekly dates, conflict-resolution exercises, etc.) can save your marriage. Most marriages end in divorce because of a cheating partner (like in the love-triangle scenario), financial hardships, addictions, or a lack of communication between partners. Divorce has become an acceptable form of resolution in faulty relationships because almost 50 percent of all new marriages end in divorce within five years. Though it may be socially acceptable, perhaps it would be easier for you to take time dating around for a while and figuring out what type of person you are most compatible with before deciding to marry. As popular a relationship-ending method as it may be, you will not enjoy going through a prolonged, expensive divorce if you could've avoided the disaster altogether by taking the time to carefully choose a mate that was perfect for you.

Studies have shown that the younger you are when you get married, the more likely it is for your marriage to end in divorce. If newlywed eighty-year-old couples can be used as an example, then it is never too late for marriage! Do not convert a bad relationship into a marriage just because you believe a piece of paper legally binding you to your partner will make your love suddenly "work."

Mental Illness

Your depression and other mood disorders can stem from emotional conflict if you are in the wrong type of relationship. Many people don't know how to express themselves in conflicts, and the result is a term known as anger-turned-inward.

Anger-turned-inward is often found to be at the root of a depressive state when you are in a dysfunctional relationship. It can happen when you take the anger you have for the issues in your relationship and turn it inward toward yourself. You may believe you are the cause of the difficulties in your relationship or that you are helpless to change the current situation.

Perhaps your partner has cheated on you, picked arguments with you, or has hit you when he/she was angry. You are shocked and enraged by what they've done, but because you want to resolve whatever problems you and your partner are facing, or because you have low self-esteem and believe you don't deserve any better, you turn the anger inward toward yourself.

Thus, giving yourself an emotional beating all the time can then lead you to the clinical feeling of depression.

Occupational Issues

Stress, fighting, and other issues stemming from bad relationships can lead one to having sleep and appetite disturbances with resultant decreased energy and concentration. With this, your productivity and performance in the workplace may be impacted, causing you to lose your job or even keeping you from being promoted to a higher-paying position.

How about if your relationship at home with your partner is so bad that you decide to cheat on him/her with a co-worker? It may only feel natural. You see this co-worker every day. Gradually, you become more familiar with him/her until you've formed a deep emotional bond that may lead to sex—even sex on the job. You may be discovered and fired, or other co-workers may find out about your affair and pass this information onto your partner. This signals trouble.

Problems with Your Immediate Family

Your family usually knows when there are problems in your life. To avoid admitting that you are having relationship problems, you might begin to isolate yourself or behave differently. Your family can likely sense that something is wrong. When questioned, you might prefer to deny that you have problems within your relationship. This may cause a rift between you and your immediate family. Your family may grow frustrated with the fact that you don't want to be honest with them when they are only trying to help you. Your bond with your family can be weakened to the point where your communication becomes infrequent. You can also lose their respect, since you have failed to share with them the vulnerabilities of your relationship.

Furthermore, your family's sixth sense about your emotional anguish can sharpen when you are in a relationship that is abusive. If you suddenly stop wanting to see or spend time with your family because you "have to" spend time with your partner, they know this isn't normal. If you're not allowed to reach out to them, they will notice the change of behavior. Your family will be rooting for you to leave him/her, but if you disregard your family's encouragement out of fear of that abusive partner, your family may see this as you willingly wanting to be in this dysfunctional relationship, and they may subsequently stop reaching out to help you.

Educational Problems

If you are in school and are involved in the wrong type of relationship, your grades can drop significantly. It can become difficult to concentrate in school on tests or other projects. How quickly do we forget that being in and out of love can lead to academic difficulty? Therefore, all students, both young and old, must keep in mind that being in the wrong type of relationship can make it difficult to concentrate on your schoolwork.

Sleeping with the Enemy

Dear Dr. O,

My husband is physically abusive to me. After a night of hitting me or arguing, he wants to be intimate, which includes sex. I am afraid to say no. What should I do?

Mrs. Y,

Texas.

Dear Mrs. Y,

First, you have to seek out help and gradually remove yourself from this type of situation. I applaud you for sharing your story, because I am sure there are many others in the same or similar position. Mrs. Y, plan your exit from this abusive relationship. Don't move too quickly, as he may become more intense and aggressive if he suspects that you are trying to leave him. The bottom line is that you must remove yourself from this situation. If you are just too afraid that your spouse will physically attack you when you attempt to leave, have the local police escort you off the premises. They are trained to handle this type of situation.

Dr. O.

Dear Readers,

Do you have any more suggestions for our friend, Mrs. Y? If so, leave a comment for her and others who are "sleeping with the enemy." Readers, she really needs to hear from you!

If you are not happy with your relationship go to: www. AskDrO.com

Stay or Leave?

"Should I stay in an abusive relationship?" This is a question that many people have faced at one time or another—perhaps you have wondered it yourself. The second question that many people have is, "Can I afford to live independently?" In today's harsh economic times, the answer is usually no. Another issue is how to participate in sex with an abusive mate. This is a very difficult feat that many people have learned to accomplish, but the harsh reality is that sex against one's will is simply *rape*. Staying in an abusive relationship is not what the doctor ordered and can certainly lead to depression and/or anxiety disorders.

If you are not convinced that you need to leave an abusive relationship immediately, then write down the risks and the benefits of staying versus leaving. I bet you that your piece of paper will be covered with the benefits of leaving this abusive relationship. Sure, you may be set back financially, but the loss of financial security results in the gain of self-confidence, peace of mind, freedom from physical abuse, relaxation in a place of your own. Plan your exit and be quick and deliberate.

1. Accept the fact that you are in an abusive and unhealthy relationship. You have control to stop the cycle. You may begin to experience anxiety, depression, and worry when you are planning your escape from this relationship, but you must flee.

2. Establish your own bank account at a different bank independent of your partner.

3. Search the home for any weapons (i.e. guns and knives) and remove them when the abusive partner is not at home.

4. Don't go to the first place your abusive partner will look. This usually includes a family member's or close friend's home. Exercise caution and discretion. You (and your children if you have some) may have to spend a few weeks or months in a hideaway shelter to ensure your safety.

5. If you have children, make sure there are schools in the area you escape to so that there will not be a break in your children's education.

6. Speak with a spiritual counselor if you need that added support. A local psychiatrist or therapist may also be helpful.

7. If you have children, ask them whether they would like to speak to a psychiatrist about the new change in their lives.

8. Fight the urge to return to your partner because you may be feeling guilty and depressed about him/her not seeing the kids or about leaving him/her with no warning.

9. Do not answer his/her calls.

10. If you do end up answering his/her calls, do not tell them of your whereabouts. If you aren't sure whether you will be able to resist your abusive partner's cries or pleas for you to come back, change your cell-phone number!

11. Don't jump into a new relationship soon after leaving this abusive one; take some time to process and review how and when your previous relationship became abusive and what you need to do to repair yourself emotionally, mentally, physically, and spiritually before adding your issues to someone else's life.

12. Besides work, do other things to keep your mind occupied. With your children, participate in activities like bowling, going to the zoo or museum, etc., so they understand that the problems in your relationship with their father or mother will not affect your relationship with them.

13. Test yourself physically. After an abusive relationship, you may feel vulnerable or powerless, perhaps because you are afraid your spouse will find you and harm you, or because the power you once felt over your own body and

safety is now gone. Consider taking karate, kick-boxing, or self-defense classes to regain your sense of power. Test yourself by registering for a marathon.

Once you've practiced for months and have finally reached the finish line, you can feel accomplished in having shown yourself that you will be a survivor to any physical and/or mental hardship.

I hope these thirteen steps will help you make a safe exit from your abusive relationship and aid you in overcoming the negative emotions you feel after being in such a situation.

Enough said,

Dr. O.

Strategies to Avoid Relationship Pitfalls

- Don't rush into any new relationship. Let things progress slowly and naturally.

- Ask very specific questions about this new person's past relationships and breakups.

- If the new situation you are in feels wrong or potentially dangerous, don't force it, no matter how lonely you are at the time.

- If you have sex with this new partner, *always* protect yourself until you are in a serious, committed relationship.

- Set boundaries in the beginning (i.e. average number of phone calls per day, average amount of time he/she can come visit you at home or at work, etc.).

- Spend time around them and their family. If they are rude or inconsiderate to their own family, they will most likely treat you similarly.

- If they have children, spend time interacting with them.

- If you don't understand any aspect of your new partner's behavior, cautiously inquire about it.

- *Do not* engage in mortgage, co-signatures, bank loans, etc. with your partner until you are married.

- Always maintain your own bank account, even after you and your partner marry. Be open and honest about this condition with your mate.Do not force your children on the new mate. Yes, you are a package deal, but remember that everyone does not want gravy with their grits at the first meal.

Relationship Examples

A. Mrs. J has been calling her husband during the day only to get his voicemail. When she confronts him about this issue, he becomes very angry and leaves home for several days. She has been crying and troubled by his actions for the last couple of months.

    1. What type of relationship might she be currently in?

    2. What should she do if this continues?

    3. Is this type of problem common among your friends?

B. John was abused by his ex-wife. He meets Sue at a workshop for social workers. After talking to her for a while, he realizes that she is also a divorcee. They both had similar experiences in their previous relationships. The conversation between the two of them at the conference was warm and inviting.

    1. What should they do about their initial feelings?

    2. What type of relationship are they at risk of developing?

3. Is therapy recommended for one or both individuals?

Now, students, I have taken you through a rigorous course on love. Perhaps you read this during a plane ride, bathroom visit, or in-office sneaky breaks. You should be equipped with the following:

- Information for relationship survival in the twenty-first century
- A handbook for things to do and not to do in your next relationship
- And finally, the tools to get out of a bad relationship

Remember there is more to come in the next volume, so stay tuned and keep that heart and those ears open.

Thanks,

Professor Love a.k.a. Dr. O.

Index

CPSIA information can be obtained at www.ICGtesting.com
Printed in the USA
LVOW061203311012

305186LV00001B/3/P